Dogs

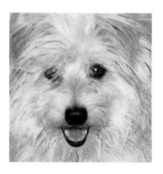

Written by Nicki Saltis

Photography by Michael Curtain

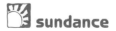 sundance

HAWTHORNE

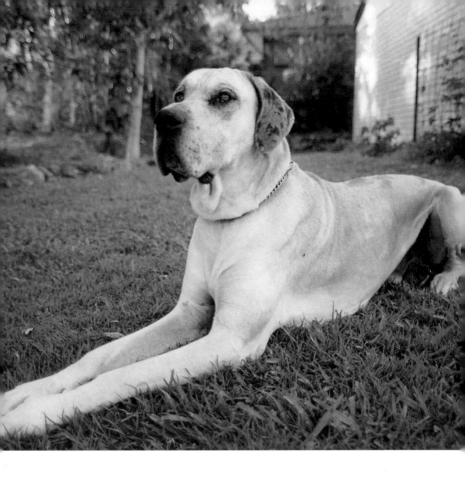

This is a big dog.

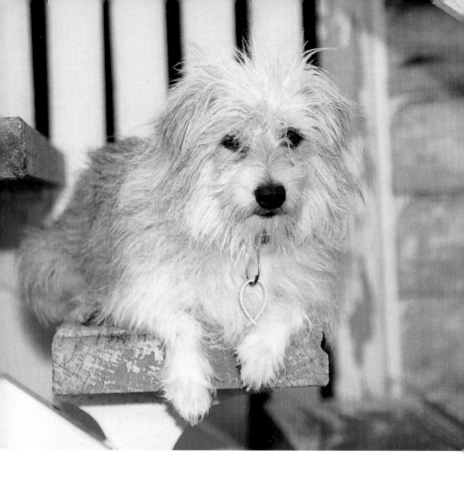

This is a little dog.

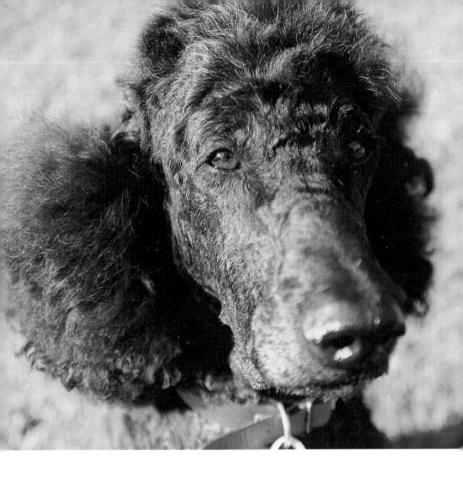

This is a black dog.

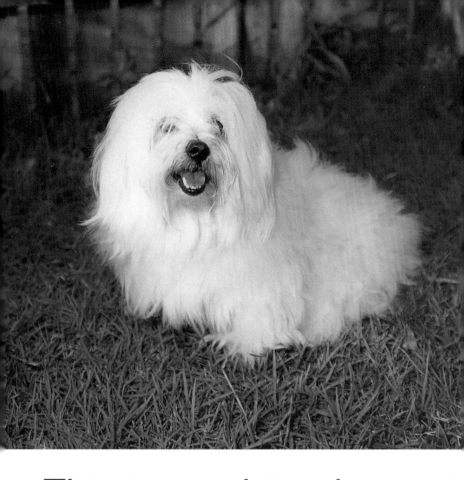

This is a white dog.

HAWTHORNE

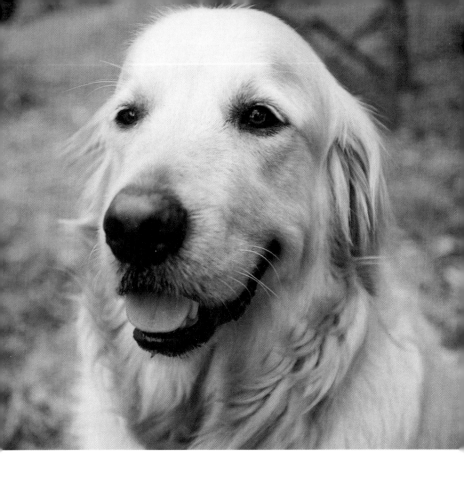

This is a happy dog.

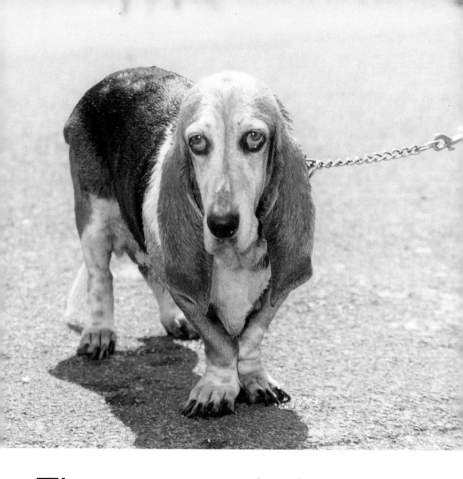

This is a sad dog.

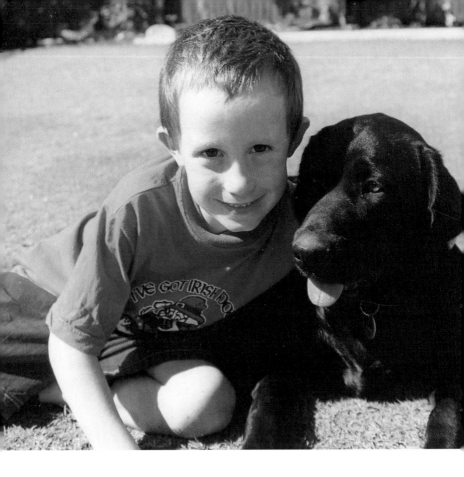

This is my dog!

HAWTHORNE